GW00569933

PLATE 1

Test Pattern

PLATE 2

Test Pattern

PLATE 3

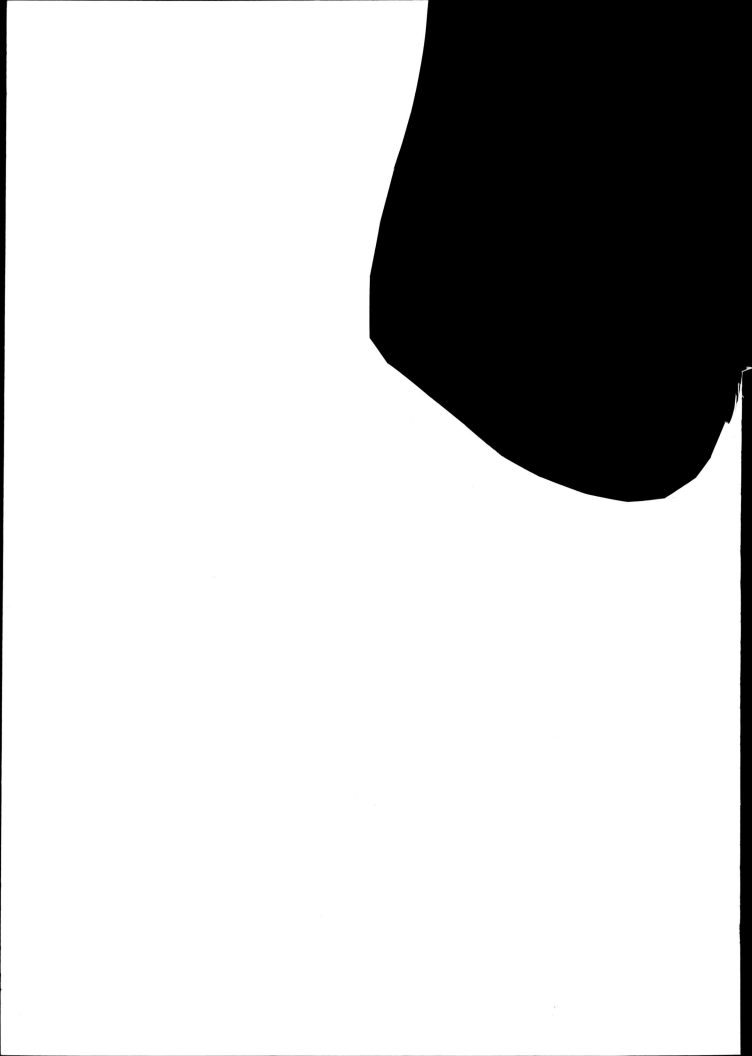

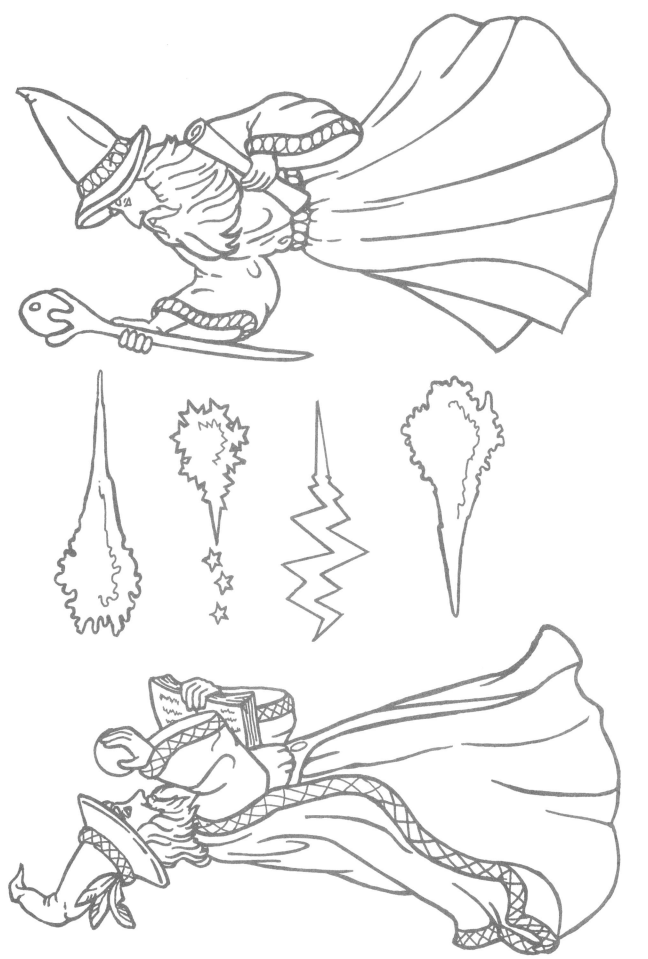

PLATE 5

Test Pattern

PLATE 6

PLATE 7

PLATE 8

Choose a spell for the wizard by cutting out the center of his "bubble" and one of the designs on the left. Following the instructions on the inside back cover, place the wizard face down on your surface, then arrange the spell inside the "bubble."

PLATE 9

PLATE 10

PLATE 11

Test Pattern

Plate 12

Test Pattern

PLATE 13

Test Pattern

PLATE 14

Test Pattern

PLATE 15

Test Pattern

PLATE 18

Test Pattern

PLATE 19

Test Pattern

PLATE 20

Test Pattern

PLATE 21

Test Pattern

PLATE 22

PLATE 23

PLATE 24

BOOK 3

POP, ROCK 'N BLUES

ポップ・ロックン・ブルース

by

Jane Smisor Bastien

GWM

General Words & Music Co. — Neil A. Kjos, Jr., Publishers

ISBN 0-8497-6036-4

PREFACE

Pop, Rock 'N Blues, Book 3, consists of seven compositions designed to introduce the pianist to the styles and sounds of today's music. The pieces are suitable for supplementary assignment and recital repertoire.

Although the compositions are set in the approximate order of difficulty, the teacher and student may wish to choose the order rather than proceeding in the sequence presented.

Pop, Rock 'N Blues, Book 3, is approximately LEVEL FOUR in the **"Music Through The Piano"** series.

Additional **"Music Through The Piano"** materials to be correlated with **Pop, Rock 'N Blues, Book 3,** include:

BOOKS:

Piano Literature, Volumes 1, 2, 3

Major Scales and Pieces

Minor Scales and Pieces

Czerny and Hanon

SOLOS:

March of the Troll Dolls

July 4th Square Dance

Final Exam Blues

Space Explorers

CONTENTS

			Page
New Orleans Blues.......	ニューオリーンズブルース		4
Walkin'.....................	歩きましょう		6
Goin' Home	家に帰ろう		8
8 O'clock Rock	8時のロック		10
Blue Monday	ゆううつな月曜日		12
High on a Windy Hill....	風の吹く丘		14
Funky Night	こわい夜		16

New Orleans Blues

ニューオリーンズブルース

Moderately, with a steady beat

Walkin'

歩きましょう

Goin' Home

家に帰ろう

Moderately slowly, with expression

GP-39

8 o'clock Rock

8時のロック

Blue Monday

ゆううつな月曜日

High on a Windy Hill

風の吹く丘

Funky Night

こわい夜